Word Bird's

Rainy-Day Dance

Published in the United States of America by The Child's World®, Inc.
PO Box 326
Chanhassen, MN 55317-0326
800-599-READ
www.childsworld.com

Project Manager Mary Berendes
Editor Katherine Stevenson, Ph.D.
Designer Ian Butterworth

Library of Congress Cataloging-in-Publication Data
Moncure, Jane Belk.
Word Bird's rainy-day dance / by Jane Belk Moncure.
p. cm.
Summary: Word Bird and his classmates perform a play showing how
seeds, sun, and rain combine to produce growing plants.
ISBN 1-56766-893-3 (lib. : alk. paper)
[1. Gardening—Fiction. 2. Schools—Fiction.
3. Birds—Fiction. 4. Animals—Fiction.]   I. Title.
PZ7.M739 Wop 2002
[E]—dc21
2001006054

Word Bird's

Rainy-Day Dance

by Jane Belk Moncure

illustrated by Chris McEwan

One rainy day Miss Beary said,
"Let's dance a rainy-day story dance.
Who wants to be a farmer?"

"I do," said Word Bird.
"I will be the farmer in our dance."

"I will be a carrot," said Bunny.

"I will be an apple tree," said Mouse.

"I will be a flower," said Cat.

"Now we need raindrops for
 our story dance," said Word Bird.
"We will be raindrops," said Frog
 and Duck.

"Are we ready?" asked Frog.
"Wait," said Word Bird. "We need
sunshine for our story dance."

"I will be the sunshine," said Pig.
"I will do a sunshine dance."

"The rest of us will be the wind,"
said Miss Beary. "We will blow
the raindrops."

Word Bird made a stage with blocks.
Then Word Bird called Bunny, Mouse,
and Cat to the stage.

"Here we go," said Word Bird.
"The farmer plows the ground and
plants seeds—one by one."

Word Bird gave Bunny, Mouse,
and Cat each a pat on the head.
They curled up on the floor.

"The farmer rakes the ground,"
said Word Bird. Bunny giggled.
Mouse giggled, too.

"And the farmer pulls the weeds,"
   Word Bird said. Word Bird pulled
   Cat's tail, just a tiny bit. Cat giggled.
"I'm not a weed," Cat said.

"Now it is our turn," said Frog
and Duck. "We are raindrops.
Drip-drop. Drip-drop."

Frog jumped over the seeds.
"The rain is raining all around,"
Frog sang.

"It rains on the farmer's field," said Duck.
"And it makes mud puddles."

"The wind blows the raindrops,"
said Frog. Everyone blew. Frog
nearly fell over.

"The little seeds pop out of the ground," said Word Bird. Bunny, Mouse, and Cat popped up.

"It is my turn," said Pig.
"The sun shines on the little plants."
Pig danced on tiptoes until . . .

the big, yellow hat fell off and
rolled away. "Oh dear," said Pig,
running after it.

"Keep dancing," said Word Bird.
Bunny stood up on tiptoes.

"Now I am a crunchy carrot, thanks to the rain and sun," Bunny said.

"I am a tree," said Mouse. "I will keep
  growing until I have big juicy apples."
"And I am a flower, blowing in the
  wind," said Cat.

As the story dance came to an end,
Word Bird said, "First came the
raindrops, then came the sun, . . .

and the little plants grew
one by one. The end."

"You did such a good story dance,"
said Miss Beary. "I think we will have . .

a bubble party for a rainy-day treat.
Blow lots and lots of bubbles!"
And everyone did.

Can you read these words with Word Bird?

rainy

blocks

farmer

stage

carrot

seeds

apple tree

weeds

flower

mud puddles

raindrops

plants

sunshine

bubbles

wind